by Liz Marsham

MAD LIBS
An imprint of Penguin Random House LLC, New York

First published in the United States of America by Mad Libs,
an imprint of Penguin Random House LLC, New York, 2022

Mad Libs format copyright © 2022 by Penguin Random House LLC

Concept created by Roger Price & Leonard Stern

Cover illustration by Jessica Doize

Visit us online at penguinrandomhouse.com.

Printed in the United States of America

ISBN 9780593519684
1 3 5 7 9 10 8 6 4 2
COMR

MAD LIBS

INSTRUCTIONS

MAD LIBS® is a game for people who don't like games!
It can be played by one, two, three, four, or forty.

• RIDICULOUSLY SIMPLE DIRECTIONS

In this tablet you will find stories containing blank spaces where words
are left out. One player, the READER, selects one of these stories. The
READER does not tell anyone what the story is about. Instead, he/she asks
the other players, the WRITERS, to give him/her words. These words are
used to fill in the blank spaces in the story.

• TO PLAY

The READER asks each WRITER in turn to call out a word—an adjective or
a noun or whatever the space calls for—and uses them to fill in the blank
spaces in the story. The result is a MAD LIBS® game.

When the READER then reads the completed MAD LIBS® game to the other
players, they will discover that they have written a story that is fantastic,
screamingly funny, shocking, silly, crazy, or just plain dumb—depending
upon which words each WRITER called out.

• EXAMPLE (*Before* and *After*)

"_____!" he said _____
　　　　　EXCLAMATION　　　　　　　　　　　　　　ADVERB

as he jumped into his convertible _____ and
　　　　　　　　　　　　　　　　　　　　　　NOUN

drove off with his _____ wife.
　　　　　　　　　　ADJECTIVE

"_____**OUCH**_____!" he said _____**HAPPILY**_____
　　　　　EXCLAMATION　　　　　　　　　　　　　　ADVERB

as he jumped into his convertible _____**CAT**_____ and
　　　　　　　　　　　　　　　　　　　　　　NOUN

drove off with his _____**BRAVE**_____ wife.
　　　　　　　　　　ADJECTIVE

QUICK REVIEW

In case you have forgotten what adjectives, adverbs, nouns, and verbs are, here is a quick review:

An ADJECTIVE describes something or somebody. *Lumpy, soft, ugly, messy,* and *short* are adjectives.

An ADVERB tells how something is done. It modifies a verb and usually ends in "ly." *Modestly, stupidly, greedily,* and *carefully* are adverbs.

A NOUN is the name of a person, place, or thing. *Sidewalk, umbrella, bridle, bathtub,* and *nose* are nouns.

A VERB is an action word. *Run, pitch, jump,* and *swim* are verbs. Put the verbs in past tense if the directions say PAST TENSE. *Ran, pitched, jumped,* and *swam* are verbs in the past tense.

When we ask for A PLACE, we mean any sort of place: a country or city (*Spain, Cleveland*) or a room (*bathroom, kitchen*).

An EXCLAMATION or SILLY WORD is any sort of funny sound, gasp, grunt, or outcry, like *Wow!, Ouch!, Whomp!, Ick!,* and *Gadzooks!*

When we ask for specific words, like a NUMBER, a COLOR, an ANIMAL, or a PART OF THE BODY, we mean a word that is one of those things, like *seven, blue, horse,* or *head.*

When we ask for a PLURAL, it means more than one. For example, *cat* pluralized is *cats.*

MAD LIBS® is fun to play with friends, but you can also play it by yourself! To begin with, DO NOT look at the story on the page below. Fill in the blanks on this page with the words called for. Then, using the words you have selected, fill in the blank spaces in the story.

Now you've created your own hilarious MAD LIBS® game!

IS IT THURSDAY YET?

NOUN _____

PLURAL NOUN _____

CITY _____

OCCUPATION _____

COLOR _____

SILLY WORD _____

PLURAL NOUN _____

NUMBER _____

TYPE OF LIQUID _____

EXCLAMATION _____

PART OF THE BODY _____

ARTICLE OF CLOTHING _____

VERB _____

SOMETHING ALIVE _____

PART OF THE BODY _____

ADJECTIVE _____

PLURAL NOUN _____

PLURAL NOUN _____

MAD LIBS®

IS IT THURSDAY YET?

We're here in the Critical Role studio, and the _____ is about
                                                    NOUN

to begin. Everyone takes their _____ around the big game
                                  PLURAL NOUN

table. Ashley is dialing in from _____ after finishing hours of
                                    CITY

_____ work. Marisha compliments Taliesin on his bright
   OCCUPATION

_____ hair, and he chuckles at her "Sleeves Are _____"
   COLOR   SILLY WORD

shirt. Laura is halfway through rolling her favorite _____ –
                                                        PLURAL NOUN

all _____ of them. Sam fills his giant flask with _____
      NUMBER   TYPE OF LIQUID

and takes off his jacket. " _____ , is that a picture of me?"
                              EXCLAMATION

Liam asks. Sure enough, Liam's _____ is printed right there
                                  PART OF THE BODY

on Sam's _____. Right before the cameras _____,
           ARTICLE OF CLOTHING   VERB

Travis tries to make Matt laugh. " _____ _____!"
                                     SOMETHING ALIVE   PART OF THE BODY

Travis shouts. But Matt just smiles at the camera and says, "Welcome

to Critical Role, where a bunch of us _____ voice actors sit
                                         ADJECTIVE

around and play _____ & _____!"
                  PLURAL NOUN   PLURAL NOUN

MAD LIBS® is fun to play with friends, but you can also play it by yourself! To begin with, DO NOT look at the story on the page below. Fill in the blanks on this page with the words called for. Then, using the words you have selected, fill in the blank spaces in the story.

Now you've created your own hilarious MAD LIBS® game!

A WORD FROM OUR SPONSOR

SILLY WORD _____

PLURAL NOUN _____

ADJECTIVE _____

PART OF THE BODY _____

ANIMAL (PLURAL) _____

VERB _____

NUMBER _____

NOUN _____

TYPE OF FOOD _____

TYPE OF FOOD _____

TYPE OF LIQUID _____

ADJECTIVE _____

PLURAL NOUN _____

ARTICLE OF CLOTHING _____

VERB _____

NOUN _____

Matt: Before we get started, our sponsor tonight is _____,
SILLY WORD

makers of fine _____.
PLURAL NOUN

Sam: On my way here, I was thinking, how do I do this _____
ADJECTIVE

sponsor justice, and—

Travis: Wait, Sam, what are those things biting your _____?
PART OF THE BODY

Sam: _____!
ANIMAL (PLURAL)

Laura: How much does that _____, on a scale of one to ten?
VERB

Sam: _____!
NUMBER

Marisha: Why do you even have those?

Sam: Oh, they live in my _____. Anyway, time to mix
NOUN

some _____ with this _____, and . . . Ashley, do you
TYPE OF FOOD   TYPE OF FOOD

have the _____ gun ready?
TYPE OF LIQUID

Ashley: Yeah, let me just get my _____ goggles on.
ADJECTIVE

Taliesin (singing): *Oh beautiful, for spacious* _____—
PLURAL NOUN

Sam: No, Taliesin, the song comes *after* I take off my _____!
ARTICLE OF CLOTHING

Liam: Sam, how does this _____ the sponsor?
VERB

Sam: Well, that's all the _____ we have. Back to you, Matt!
NOUN

MAD LIBS® is fun to play with friends, but you can also play it by yourself! To begin with, DO NOT look at the story on the page below. Fill in the blanks on this page with the words called for. Then, using the words you have selected, fill in the blank spaces in the story.

Now you've created your own hilarious MAD LIBS® game!

MEET VOX MACHINA

PART OF THE BODY (PLURAL) _____

A PLACE _____

PERSON IN ROOM _____

ADJECTIVE _____

NOUN _____

PLURAL NOUN _____

NOUN _____

SOMETHING ALIVE _____

VERB (PAST TENSE) _____

NOUN _____

TYPE OF LIQUID _____

NOUN _____

PLURAL NOUN _____

PLURAL NOUN _____

VERB _____

VERB ENDING IN "ING" _____

EXCLAMATION _____

VERB _____

MAD LIBS®

MEET VOX MACHINA

I was once lucky enough to witness Vox Machina with my very own

_____. Yes, the saviors of (the) _____, just as
PART OF THE BODY (PLURAL)   A PLACE

close to me as you are now, _____. First into battle were the
                              PERSON IN ROOM

_____ twins, Vex and Vax, scouting the _____ ahead.
ADJECTIVE   NOUN

The stealthy Vax circled behind his enemies, ready to throw his deadly

_____. Vex, the tracker, nocked an arrow into her
PLURAL NOUN

_____ and took aim. Then Grog, the hulking half- _____,
NOUN   SOMETHING ALIVE

_____ onto the battlefield, swinging his _____.
VERB (PAST TENSE)   NOUN

His targets ran, but Keyleth used her nature magic to summon waves

of _____ and walls of _____ to block their path.
TYPE OF LIQUID   NOUN

Loud bangs echoed as the gunslinger, Percy, fired his _____.
                                                       PLURAL NOUN

Meanwhile, Scanlan sang magical _____ to _____ his
                                 PLURAL NOUN   VERB

enemies. And Pike the healer brought up the rear, ready to _____
                                                            VERB

her friends if they got in trouble. Sure, all that _____
                                                    VERB ENDING IN "ING"

totally wrecked my store. But _____, it was worth it to
                              EXCLAMATION

_____ my heroes.
VERB

MAD LIBS® is fun to play with friends, but you can also play it by yourself! To begin with, DO NOT look at the story on the page below. Fill in the blanks on this page with the words called for. Then, using the words you have selected, fill in the blank spaces in the story.

Now you've created your own hilarious MAD LIBS® game!

WHAT'S IN THE BAG, GROG?

A PLACE _____

PLURAL NOUN _____

ADJECTIVE _____

CITY _____

PLURAL NOUN _____

PLURAL NOUN _____

ADJECTIVE _____

CELEBRITY _____

ARTICLE OF CLOTHING _____

TYPE OF FOOD _____

NUMBER _____

COLOR _____

VERB (PAST TENSE) _____

VERB _____

ADVERB _____

SAME TYPE OF FOOD _____

MAD LIBS®

WHAT'S IN THE BAG, GROG?

A demon locked Vox Machina in (the) _____! To open the
_{A PLACE}

door, they needed to leave an offering on a plate . . . "Grog," said Vex,

"what about some of the _____ from your bag?"
_{PLURAL NOUN}

Grog reached into the magical bag and pulled out:

- Ten _____ swords
  _{ADJECTIVE}

- Two _____ guards' shields
  _{CITY}

- Twelve shiny _____
  _{PLURAL NOUN}

- Six sticky _____
  _{PLURAL NOUN}

- A/An _____ robe from _____'s house
  _{ADJECTIVE} _{CELEBRITY}

- A fancy _____
  _{ARTICLE OF CLOTHING}

- A battered _____
  _{TYPE OF FOOD}

Lastly, he opened his fist, and out fell _____ _____ coins.
_{NUMBER} _{COLOR}

As the last coin _____ on the plate, the door opened.
_{VERB (PAST TENSE)}

"I have to _____ *all of our stuff*?" cried Grog. "It's okay, Grog,"
_{VERB}

said Pike _____. "We can get you more." Grog sighed, "But
_{ADVERB}

that _____ looked tasty!"
_{SAME TYPE OF FOOD}

MAD LIBS® is fun to play with friends, but you can also play it by yourself! To begin with, DO NOT look at the story on the page below. Fill in the blanks on this page with the words called for. Then, using the words you have selected, fill in the blank spaces in the story.

Now you've created your own hilarious MAD LIBS® game!

AN AUTOMATON'S BEST FRIEND

TYPE OF BUILDING _____

PLURAL NOUN _____

VERB (PAST TENSE) _____

NOUN _____

CITY _____

VERB _____

PART OF THE BODY _____

VERB ENDING IN "ING" _____

FIRST NAME _____

SILLY WORD _____

NOUN _____

VERB _____

ARTICLE OF CLOTHING _____

VERB (PAST TENSE) _____

PART OF THE BODY _____

EXCLAMATION _____

NOUN _____

VERB ENDING IN "ING" _____

Percy and Tary were hard at work in Percy's _____, building

TYPE OF BUILDING

an automaton out of spare _____. Gilmore _____

PLURAL NOUN   VERB (PAST TENSE)

in, holding a crystal shaped like a/an _____. "I bring you the

NOUN

finest enchantment in _____," Gilmore proclaimed. "Perfect!

CITY

_____ the crystal right here," replied Percy as he opened

VERB

the automaton's _____. Gilmore slotted the crystal inside

PART OF THE BODY

the robot. "It *is* perfect," Tary said, while _____ the

VERB ENDING IN "ING"

robot's hand. "I will name it _____ _____, and it

FIRST NAME   SILLY WORD

will be Doty's most faithful _____—besides me, of course."

NOUN

Then, the crystal began to _____, and the automaton

VERB

leaped up, grabbed Tary's _____, and lifted him into the

ARTICLE OF CLOTHING

air. "Where is Doty?" the automaton _____. Percy held

VERB (PAST TENSE)

on to the automaton's _____ as it shook Tary back and

PART OF THE BODY

forth and repeated, "Where is *Doty*?" "_____!" Gilmore

EXCLAMATION

cried, dispelling the enchantment. The robot and Tary slumped to the

_____. "Next time," Percy said, _____ his

NOUN   VERB ENDING IN "ING"

head, "let's make it *less* faithful!"

MAD LIBS® is fun to play with friends, but you can also play it by yourself! To begin with, DO NOT look at the story on the page below. Fill in the blanks on this page with the words called for. Then, using the words you have selected, fill in the blank spaces in the story.

Now you've created your own hilarious MAD LIBS® game!

SCANLAN'S SONG

VERB ENDING IN "ING" _____

ADJECTIVE _____

VERB _____

NOUN _____

PLURAL NOUN _____

A PLACE _____

SOMETHING ALIVE _____

VERB _____

VERB _____

NUMBER _____

VERB _____

ADJECTIVE _____

PART OF THE BODY _____

VERB ENDING IN "ING" _____

PERSON IN ROOM _____

VERB ENDING IN "ING" _____

MAD LIBS®

SCANLAN'S SONG

Need a confidence boost before _____ that lock?
                          VERB ENDING IN "ING"

Feeling nervous, or _____, or tired?
                    ADJECTIVE

Then _____ as Scanlan sings only for you,
        VERB

and my sweet _____ will leave you inspired.
                NOUN

My rhymes enthrall _____
                    PLURAL NOUN

from Kymal to (the) _____,
                    A PLACE

I've tamed the wild _____ and more.
                  SOMETHING ALIVE

When I'm with my friends, we can even _____ gods!
                                        VERB

(Just don't ask us to _____ a door.)
                        VERB

I've made _____ skeletons fall to my might,
            NUMBER

made a fire genie _____ for its crimes.
                    VERB

But how did I best these _____ creatures, you ask?
                          ADJECTIVE

My _____ shoots lightning sometimes!
    PART OF THE BODY

Do you think your pal Scanlan is _____ with you?
                                  VERB ENDING IN "ING"

That I can't do what I said I could?

No! I *promise* you, _____, a guaranteed win!
                    PERSON IN ROOM

Now get _____, and make me look good.
        VERB ENDING IN "ING"

MAD LIBS® is fun to play with friends, but you can also play it by yourself! To begin with, DO NOT look at the story on the page below. Fill in the blanks on this page with the words called for. Then, using the words you have selected, fill in the blank spaces in the story.

Now you've created your own hilarious MAD LIBS® game!

FUN IN ALL ITS FORMS

ADJECTIVE _____

ADJECTIVE _____

PLURAL NOUN _____

VERB _____

ADJECTIVE _____

EXCLAMATION _____

ANIMAL _____

VERB (PAST TENSE) _____

TYPE OF LIQUID _____

NUMBER _____

ADJECTIVE _____

VERB ENDING IN "ING" _____

PART OF THE BODY (PLURAL) _____

SOMETHING ALIVE _____

NOUN _____

ADVERB _____

NOUN _____

FUN IN ALL ITS FORMS

In her ivory tower, Allura, a/an _____ arcanist, and her wife,

ADJECTIVE

Kima, surprised Keyleth with a present: a huge room full of moving,

_____ contraptions and shimmering _____.

ADJECTIVE   PLURAL NOUN

"Welcome to your obstacle course!" shouted Kima from across the room.

"It's so you can _____ your shape-changing magic," Allura said.

VERB

She pointed at a wall with "Smash to Start" painted in _____

ADJECTIVE

letters. " _____!" yelled Keyleth, and she transformed

EXCLAMATION

into a giant _____. She crashed through the wall and

ANIMAL

immediately _____ into a pool of _____.

VERB (PAST TENSE)   TYPE OF LIQUID

Keyleth became a/an _____-foot-long eel and swam to the other

NUMBER

side. Then _____ hammers began _____

ADJECTIVE   VERB ENDING IN "ING"

in her path! Keyleth changed into a tiny fairy with glowing

_____ and quickly flew toward the ceiling.

PART OF THE BODY (PLURAL)

A winged _____ tried to eat her, so she became a

SOMETHING ALIVE

gigantic _____ . . . and accidentally broke through the

NOUN

tower wall! "Oops!" said Keyleth _____. "Technically," Kima

ADVERB

said with a/an _____, "I think this means you won!"

NOUN

MAD LIBS® is fun to play with friends, but you can also play it by yourself! To begin with, DO NOT look at the story on the page below. Fill in the blanks on this page with the words called for. Then, using the words you have selected, fill in the blank spaces in the story.

Now you've created your own hilarious MAD LIBS® game!

PIKE'S PRAYER

NOUN _____

ADJECTIVE _____

TYPE OF LIQUID _____

PART OF THE BODY (PLURAL) _____

VERB ENDING IN "ING" _____

PLURAL NOUN _____

VERB _____

PLURAL NOUN _____

VERB _____

NOUN _____

PLURAL NOUN _____

PLURAL NOUN _____

VERB _____

ADJECTIVE _____

PLURAL NOUN _____

VERB _____

PART OF THE BODY (PLURAL) _____

ADVERB _____

MAD LIBS®

PIKE'S PRAYER

Oh, Everlight! I pray to you,

May your _____ lead my friends to their _____ desires,
　　　　　　 NOUN　　　　　　　　　　　　　　　　　ADJECTIVE

May my best buddy Grog always have _____ in his cup
　　　　　　　　　　　　　　　　　　　　　TYPE OF LIQUID

and strength in his _____,
　　　　　　　　　　 PART OF THE BODY (PLURAL)

May Vax's enemies never see him _____ and
　　　　　　　　　　　　　　　　　　VERB ENDING IN "ING"

may his _____ always know where to _____ him,
　　　　　 PLURAL NOUN　　　　　　　　　　　　　　 VERB

May Vex's _____ strike true,
　　　　　　 PLURAL NOUN

May Percy _____ the machines of his dreams,
　　　　　　　 VERB

May Keyleth lead her people with love, _____,
　　　　　　　　　　　　　　　　　　　　　　　　 NOUN

and _____,
　　　 PLURAL NOUN

May Scanlan always find new _____ to tell and new songs
　　　　　　　　　　　　　　　　 PLURAL NOUN

to _____,
　　 VERB

And may your light guide us in our _____ days and our
　　　　　　　　　　　　　　　　　　　ADJECTIVE

darkest _____.
　　　　 PLURAL NOUN

Oh, and one more thing: May we _____ our enemies'
　　　　　　　　　　　　　　　　　　VERB

_____ hard, every time. Okay. Thanks . . .
PART OF THE BODY (PLURAL)

Oh, uh, your _____ devoted servant, Pike.
　　　　　　　 ADVERB

From CRITICAL ROLE MAD LIBS® • © 2022 by Gilmore's Glorious Goods LLC. All Rights Reserved.
Published by Mad Libs, an imprint of Penguin Random House LLC, 2022

MAD LIBS® is fun to play with friends, but you can also play it by yourself! To begin with, DO NOT look at the story on the page below. Fill in the blanks on this page with the words called for. Then, using the words you have selected, fill in the blank spaces in the story.

Now you've created your own hilarious MAD LIBS® game!

THE BEST BEDTIME STORY

PLURAL NOUN _____

VERB _____

ADJECTIVE _____

PLURAL NOUN _____

NOUN _____

CITY _____

ADVERB _____

PLURAL NOUN _____

VERB (PAST TENSE) _____

NUMBER _____

ADVERB _____

PLURAL NOUN _____

VERB ENDING IN "ING" _____

ADJECTIVE _____

VERB (PAST TENSE) _____

ADJECTIVE _____

SOMETHING ALIVE _____

MAD LIBS®

THE BEST BEDTIME STORY

Vex and Vax tucked their half sister Velora into bed, pulling the

_____ up under her chin. "I'm not sleepy. Will you
    PLURAL NOUN

_____ me a story?" asked Velora. "How about the time we
    VERB

rescued the _____ princess?" Vax replied. Excited, Velora's
    ADJECTIVE

eyes lit up like she had _____ in them. But then Vex said
    PLURAL NOUN

quickly, "I'm not sure that's a good _____ for bedtime."
    NOUN

Too late! Vax had already started the story: "Her kidnappers took her

to a house in _____. I crept in _____ through
    CITY   ADVERB

the window—" "Setting off a trap that shot _____,"
    PLURAL NOUN

Vex interrupted, "which _____ Vax so badly." "Then
    VERB (PAST TENSE)

_____ kidnappers rushed in," Vax cried, "and I had to act
    NUMBER

_____! I was throwing _____!" "And I
    ADVERB   PLURAL NOUN

was _____ arrows!" shouted Vex, jumping on the
    VERB ENDING IN "ING"

bed. "Then we grabbed the princess," said Vax, wrapping Velora in

a/an _____ hug. "And we _____ away!"
    ADJECTIVE   VERB (PAST TENSE)

finished Vex. The twins looked down at Velora's _____
    ADJECTIVE

face. The story worked. She was sleeping like a/an _____.
    SOMETHING ALIVE

MAD LIBS® is fun to play with friends, but you can also play it by yourself! To begin with, DO NOT look at the story on the page below. Fill in the blanks on this page with the words called for. Then, using the words you have selected, fill in the blank spaces in the story.

Now you've created your own hilarious MAD LIBS® game!

HOW DO YOU WANT TO DO THIS?

SILLY WORD _____

PLURAL NOUN _____

NOUN _____

VERB ENDING IN "ING" _____

ADJECTIVE _____

ADVERB _____

YOUR NAME _____

NOUN _____

ADJECTIVE _____

VERB _____

NUMBER _____

VERB _____

PLURAL NOUN _____

TYPE OF CONTAINER _____

TYPE OF LIQUID _____

PART OF THE BODY _____

VERB _____

NOUN _____

MAD⊙LIBS®
HOW DO YOU WANT TO DO THIS?

The battle against the mighty _____, conqueror of a
                                    SILLY WORD

thousand _____, has been raging for over an hour. Liam is
            PLURAL NOUN

hiding under the _____. Marisha is _____
                        NOUN   VERB ENDING IN "ING"

on her chair. Everyone at the table knows that Vox Machina will need

_____ help to win this fight. Then Matt looks off camera and
   ADJECTIVE

waves _____ at you. " _____," he says, "come
          ADVERB   YOUR NAME

here and pull up a/an _____! You're our _____
                            NOUN   ADJECTIVE

guest for this episode!" Soon, it's your turn, and you nervously

_____ your dice. Natural _____! "So," Matt asks you,
    VERB   NUMBER

"how do you want to _____ this?"
                          VERB

You consider your options:

•   Bury it under some _____
                            PLURAL NOUN

•   Trap it in a big _____
                        TYPE OF CONTAINER

•   Pour _____ onto its _____
            TYPE OF LIQUID   PART OF THE BODY

You make your choice, and the players _____ in excitement.
                                            VERB

It's a good thing you were here to save the _____!
                                                NOUN

From CRITICAL ROLE MAD LIBS® • © 2022 by Gilmore's Glorious Goods LLC. All Rights Reserved.
Published by Mad Libs, an imprint of Penguin Random House LLC, 2022

MAD LIBS® is fun to play with friends, but you can also play it by yourself! To begin with, DO NOT look at the story on the page below. Fill in the blanks on this page with the words called for. Then, using the words you have selected, fill in the blank spaces in the story.

Now you've created your own hilarious MAD LIBS® game!

WELCOME TO THE MIGHTY NEIN! PART 1

OCCUPATION _____

ADJECTIVE _____

TYPE OF FOOD _____

VERB _____

VERB ENDING IN "ING" _____

SOMETHING ALIVE _____

VERB _____

PART OF THE BODY _____

EXCLAMATION _____

ADJECTIVE _____

ADJECTIVE _____

VERB ENDING IN "ING" _____

TYPE OF LIQUID _____

SILLY WORD _____

ANIMAL _____

ADJECTIVE _____

NOUN _____

MAD LIBS®
WELCOME TO
THE MIGHTY NEIN! PART 1

Jester's a/an _____ who likes _____ sweets.
OCCUPATION   ADJECTIVE

Just ask, and she'll give you _____ to _____.
TYPE OF FOOD   VERB

Fjord is a spell- _____ warrior!
VERB ENDING IN "ING"

And something to know:

A godlike _____'s chasing him, so . . .
SOMETHING ALIVE

Let's _____ on to Beau,
VERB

who fights with _____ and with fist.
PART OF THE BODY

Her diplomacy's great, but _____,
EXCLAMATION

don't get her _____.
ADJECTIVE

And here's _____ Veth,
ADJECTIVE

who likes _____ her day
VERB ENDING IN "ING"

with family, theft, and a nice crisp _____.
TYPE OF LIQUID

There's arcanist Caleb, and _____, his _____.
SILLY WORD   ANIMAL

You say he smells _____? Well . . . don't tell him that.
ADJECTIVE

CONTINUED ON NEXT _____ . . .
NOUN

MAD LIBS® is fun to play with friends, but you can also play it by yourself! To begin with, DO NOT look at the story on the page below. Fill in the blanks on this page with the words called for. Then, using the words you have selected, fill in the blank spaces in the story.

Now you've created your own hilarious MAD LIBS® game!

WELCOME TO
THE MIGHTY NEIN! PART 2

NUMBER _____

VERB ENDING IN "ING" _____

SOMETHING ALIVE (PLURAL) _____

NOUN _____

ADJECTIVE _____

NOUN _____

VERB _____

OCCUPATION _____

ADJECTIVE _____

NOUN _____

VERB (PAST TENSE) _____

NUMBER _____

NOUN _____

VERB _____

PART OF THE BODY _____

ADJECTIVE _____

MAD LIBS
WELCOME TO
THE MIGHTY NEIN! PART 2

Now _____ more of this _____ party do remain,
     NUMBER   VERB ENDING IN "ING"

and many _____ they have slain.
           SOMETHING ALIVE (PLURAL)

That brawler near the _____ is Yasha, she's easy to gauge;
              NOUN

if you start a/an _____ _____,
           ADJECTIVE   NOUN

she is ready to _____!
           VERB

Caduceus the _____ is as calm as can be,
          OCCUPATION

maybe it's 'cause he drinks _____ _____ tea.
              ADJECTIVE   NOUN

Essek's an arcanist who's now on our side,

and Kingsley was Mollymauk, but then he _____.
                  VERB (PAST TENSE)

Now, there's room for _____ more
           NUMBER

at the _____ to dine,
      NOUN

so _____ your _____ down.
   VERB   PART OF THE BODY

You're in the _____ Nein!
        ADJECTIVE

MAD LIBS® is fun to play with friends, but you can also play it by yourself! To begin with, DO NOT look at the story on the page below. Fill in the blanks on this page with the words called for. Then, using the words you have selected, fill in the blank spaces in the story.

Now you've created your own hilarious MAD LIBS® game!

COOKING WITH CADUCEUS

ADJECTIVE _____

VERB _____

ANIMAL (PLURAL) _____

PLURAL NOUN _____

NOUN _____

TYPE OF FOOD _____

ADJECTIVE _____

TYPE OF LIQUID _____

TYPE OF FOOD _____

NOUN _____

ADJECTIVE _____

COLOR _____

CITY _____

ADJECTIVE _____

SOMETHING ALIVE (PLURAL) _____

TYPE OF CONTAINER _____

PLURAL NOUN _____

VERB ENDING IN "ING" _____

MAD LIBS

COOKING WITH CADUCEUS

Caduceus cooked up something ＿＿＿＿＿＿ for his friends in the
ADJECTIVE

Mighty Nein. Let's ＿＿＿＿＿＿ what's on the menu:
VERB

- For Jester, pastries shaped like ＿＿＿＿＿＿＿＿ and filled
  ANIMAL (PLURAL)

  with ＿＿＿＿＿＿
  PLURAL NOUN

- For Fjord, ＿＿＿＿＿＿＿＿ wrapped in seaweed and a big
  NOUN

  ＿＿＿＿＿＿＿＿ carved into a boat
  TYPE OF FOOD

- For Beau, ＿＿＿＿＿＿＿＿ bacon and a steaming mug of
  ADJECTIVE

  ＿＿＿＿＿＿＿＿
  TYPE OF LIQUID

- For Veth, a chest made of ＿＿＿＿＿＿＿＿ filled with pieces of
  TYPE OF FOOD

  ＿＿＿＿＿＿＿＿ cut into button shapes
  NOUN

- For Caleb, ＿＿＿＿＿＿ ＿＿＿＿＿＿ strudel, just like they
  ADJECTIVE   _COLOR_

  make in ＿＿＿＿＿＿
  CITY

- For Yasha, a stack of ＿＿＿＿＿＿ pancakes and a pile of crunchy
  ADJECTIVE

  ＿＿＿＿＿＿＿＿
  SOMETHING ALIVE (PLURAL)

As for Caduceus, he just settles back with his ＿＿＿＿＿＿＿＿＿＿
TYPE OF CONTAINER

of tea and watches his friends enjoy their ＿＿＿＿＿＿＿＿＿＿.
PLURAL NOUN

Happy ＿＿＿＿＿＿＿＿, Mighty Nein!
VERB ENDING IN "ING"

From CRITICAL ROLE MAD LIBS® • © 2022 by Gilmore's Glorious Goods LLC. All Rights Reserved.
Published by Mad Libs, an imprint of Penguin Random House LLC, 2022

MAD LIBS® is fun to play with friends, but you can also play it by yourself! To begin with, DO NOT look at the story on the page below. Fill in the blanks on this page with the words called for. Then, using the words you have selected, fill in the blank spaces in the story.

Now you've created your own hilarious MAD LIBS® game!

AYE, AYE, CAPTAIN TUSKTOOTH!

NOUN _____

ADJECTIVE _____

ADVERB _____

SOMETHING ALIVE _____

SILLY WORD _____

NOUN _____

PART OF THE BODY _____

VERB _____

NOUN _____

VERB _____

PART OF THE BODY (PLURAL) _____

ADJECTIVE _____

NOUN _____

ANIMAL _____

ADJECTIVE _____

VERB _____

VERB ENDING IN "ING" _____

NUMBER _____

MAD LIBS®
AYE, AYE,
CAPTAIN TUSKTOOTH!

The Mighty Nein's ship, *The* _____ *Eater*, was sailing across
_{NOUN}

the Lucidian Ocean with Fjord, its _____ captain, standing
_{ADJECTIVE}

_____ on the prow. Suddenly, a huge _____
_{ADVERB}   _{SOMETHING ALIVE}

reared out of the water! "Hard to _____!" commanded Fjord.
_{SILLY WORD}

Orly spun the _____, and the boat crashed into the
_{NOUN}

creature's giant _____! "Should I _____
_{PART OF THE BODY}   _{VERB}

the cannons?" cried Nott. "No," Fjord replied, "the creature is caught

in the lines. It could sink the _____!" "I think it's
_{NOUN}

hurt and just wants to _____," said Caduceus. "I'll help!"
_{VERB}

Jester said, putting her _____ on the creature to
_{PART OF THE BODY (PLURAL)}

heal it. Beau and Yasha tried to untangle it from the ropes, but it was

too _____. Then Caleb cast a/an _____ to turn
_{ADJECTIVE}   _{NOUN}

it into a little _____. "Aw, now it's so _____!"
_{ANIMAL}   _{ADJECTIVE}

Jester said. "Should we _____ it as a pet?" "No more pets on the
_{VERB}

ship," said Fjord, _____ the animal overboard.
_{VERB ENDING IN "ING"}

Jester protested, "But I only have _____!"
_{NUMBER}

MAD LIBS® is fun to play with friends, but you can also play it by yourself! To begin with, DO NOT look at the story on the page below. Fill in the blanks on this page with the words called for. Then, using the words you have selected, fill in the blank spaces in the story.

Now you've created your own hilarious MAD LIBS® game!

THE CHAOS CREW
STRIKES AGAIN

ARTICLE OF CLOTHING _____

VERB _____

ADVERB _____

ADJECTIVE _____

NUMBER _____

VERB _____

EXCLAMATION _____

VERB (PAST TENSE) _____

ADJECTIVE _____

OCCUPATION _____

TYPE OF FOOD _____

VERB (PAST TENSE) _____

TYPE OF FOOD (PLURAL) _____

VERB _____

TYPE OF FOOD (PLURAL) _____

VERB (PAST TENSE) _____

The mission was very simple: Swipe the gold key from the guard's

_____. Beau would be lookout, Jester would
ARTICLE OF CLOTHING

_____ the guard, and Nott would _____ steal
VERB   ADVERB

the key. They thought nothing could go _____. But when
ADJECTIVE

they got to the guard's post next to a bakery, he had _____
NUMBER

friends with him! Jester tried to _____ them all, but one saw
VERB

Nott taking the key. "_____!" yelled the guard,
EXCLAMATION

grabbing Nott. Jester _____ a pie from the bakery
VERB (PAST TENSE)

display and smashed it in his face. The _____ guard threw a
ADJECTIVE

fresh-baked pie back at Jester, but Beau deflected it. It hit a passing

_____, who snatched a/an _____ from a nearby
OCCUPATION   TYPE OF FOOD

stand to throw, but Jester _____ a spell to topple the
VERB (PAST TENSE)

stand. The three friends ran for it, a rain of _____
TYPE OF FOOD (PLURAL)

following them. "We did _____ the key," said Beau, "but
VERB

we started a gigantic citywide food fight." "And got some free

_____!" added Jester. Nott declared, "Mission
TYPE OF FOOD (PLURAL)

_____!"
VERB (PAST TENSE)

MAD LIBS® is fun to play with friends, but you can also play it by yourself! To begin with, DO NOT look at the story on the page below. Fill in the blanks on this page with the words called for. Then, using the words you have selected, fill in the blank spaces in the story.

Now you've created your own hilarious MAD LIBS® game!

WIDOGAST'S
WONDROUS WIZARDRY

ADJECTIVE _____

NOUN _____

TYPE OF FOOD _____

NOUN _____

PART OF THE BODY _____

NOUN _____

LETTER OF THE ALPHABET _____

COLOR _____

ADVERB _____

OCCUPATION _____

CELEBRITY _____

SILLY WORD _____

VERB _____

ANIMAL (PLURAL) _____

VERB _____

TYPE OF LIQUID _____

NOUN _____

YOUR NAME _____

MAD LIBS®
WIDOGAST'S
WONDROUS WIZARDRY

Caleb Widogast hands you a copy of his latest _____
                                                    ADJECTIVE

spell to try! Here's what is written on the _____:
                                                    NOUN

1. Combine a bit of _____ with a dash of _____
                      TYPE OF FOOD   NOUN

   in your _____
            PART OF THE BODY

2. Sprinkle it on the _____ in front of you in the shape
                            NOUN

   of a/an _____
            LETTER OF THE ALPHABET

3. Wave your hands back and forth until you see _____ sparks
                                                      COLOR

4. Speak the magic words: " _____ _____
                                  ADVERB   OCCUPATION

   _____ _____!"
        CELEBRITY   SILLY WORD

You cast the spell, and the ground begins to _____. Ten
                                                    VERB

_____ appear and _____, humming a
   ANIMAL (PLURAL)   VERB

beautiful song. Then thunder booms, and _____ rains
                                              TYPE OF LIQUID

down. "This isn't quite what I had in _____," Caleb says,
                                            NOUN

"but it is impressive. Why don't we call this one _____'s
                                                      YOUR NAME

Wondrous Wizardry instead?"

MAD LIBS® is fun to play with friends, but you can also play it by yourself! To begin with, DO NOT look at the story on the page below. Fill in the blanks on this page with the words called for. Then, using the words you have selected, fill in the blank spaces in the story.

Now you've created your own hilarious MAD LIBS® game!

ALL CATS ON DECK

VERB (PAST TENSE) _____

ADJECTIVE _____

ANIMAL _____

NOUN _____

VERB ENDING IN "ING" _____

TYPE OF FOOD (PLURAL) _____

VERB _____

NOUN _____

FIRST NAME _____

SILLY WORD _____

SOMETHING ALIVE _____

CELEBRITY _____

COLOR _____

OCCUPATION _____

A SOUND _____

ADJECTIVE _____

NOUN _____

MAD LIBS®

ALL CATS ON DECK

The Mighty Nein _____ into Widogast's Nascent
                    VERB (PAST TENSE)

Nein-Sided Tower after a/an _____ day of adventuring.
                             ADJECTIVE

Frumpkin jumped off Caleb's shoulder and into the maze of

_____-size pathways between the rooms. The hundred
      ANIMAL

fey cats in this _____ needed to get _____
                     NOUN   VERB ENDING IN "ING"

fast! He sent forty of the cats to cook _____ for
                                        TYPE OF FOOD (PLURAL)

dinner, and another ten to _____ the bedrooms. A/An
                                  VERB

_____ rang in the salon, and Frumpkin sent two cats,
       NOUN

_____ and _____, to see what Caduceus,
    FIRST NAME   SILLY WORD

Caleb and Essek wanted. Two other cats named _____
                                               SOMETHING ALIVE

and _____ got the hot tub ready for Beau and Yasha. Then
       CELEBRITY

cats named _____ and _____ set out lab equipment
              COLOR   OCCUPATION

for Veth. Another cat screeched " _____!" and brought Fjord
                                    A SOUND

and Jester some predinner treats. Finally, Frumpkin ran to the salon:

_____ beds and cookies are nice, but what Caleb really
     ADJECTIVE

needed at the end of a long _____ was his cat.
                                   NOUN

MAD LIBS® is fun to play with friends, but you can also play it by yourself! To begin with, DO NOT look at the story on the page below. Fill in the blanks on this page with the words called for. Then, using the words you have selected, fill in the blank spaces in the story.

Now you've created your own hilarious MAD LIBS® game!

MOLLYMAUK SEES YOUR FUTURE

PERSON IN ROOM _____

VERB ENDING IN "ING" _____

VERB _____

NOUN _____

VERB _____

NOUN _____

OCCUPATION _____

NOUN _____

VERB _____

TYPE OF BUILDING _____

VERB (PAST TENSE) _____

VERB ENDING IN "ING" _____

EXCLAMATION _____

SOMETHING ALIVE _____

VERB _____

PLURAL NOUN _____

ADJECTIVE _____

VERB _____

MAD LIBS®
MOLLYMAUK SEES YOUR FUTURE

Well, hello, you must be _____. I'm Molly, and I hear you've
                          PERSON IN ROOM

been _____ for me. Come and _____ a seat right
        VERB ENDING IN "ING"   VERB

here, and we'll see what fate has in _____ for you! And
                                            NOUN

remember, *I* don't _____ your future; the *cards* do. So go
                          VERB

ahead and draw three from the _____. Ah, now, your first card
                                    NOUN

is the _____. This means that you are a/an _____
          OCCUPATION   NOUN

of great character, the kind that people want to _____. And
                                                      VERB

your second card is the _____. Have you recently
                              TYPE OF BUILDING

_____ something important to you? Yes, it seemed like
    VERB (PAST TENSE)

you were _____ for something. _____,
            VERB ENDING IN "ING"   EXCLAMATION

your third card is the _____! . . . No, no, it doesn't
                            SOMETHING ALIVE

necessarily _____ anything bad. Just . . . don't trust any
                  VERB

_____, all right? That's _____ advice any
    PLURAL NOUN   ADJECTIVE

time, though. Well, it was nice to _____ you, and that'll be
                                        VERB

twenty gold, please!

MAD LIBS® is fun to play with friends, but you can also play it by yourself! To begin with, DO NOT look at the story on the page below. Fill in the blanks on this page with the words called for. Then, using the words you have selected, fill in the blank spaces in the story.

Now you've created your own hilarious MAD LIBS® game!

A WALK IN THE WOODS

PART OF THE BODY _____

NOUN _____

VERB ENDING IN "ING" _____

NOUN _____

VERB (PAST TENSE) _____

NOUN _____

VERB (PAST TENSE) _____

VERB ENDING IN "ING" _____

PLURAL NOUN _____

PART OF THE BODY (PLURAL) _____

NOUN _____

VERB (PAST TENSE) _____

NUMBER _____

ADJECTIVE _____

EXCLAMATION _____

PLURAL NOUN _____

VERB _____

A WALK IN THE WOODS

Beau and Yasha were walking hand in _____ down a lovely
PART OF THE BODY

forest path. The _____ was shining through the leaves.
NOUN

The birds were _____. Love was in the _____.
VERB ENDING IN "ING"   NOUN

Suddenly, Beau _____ Yasha behind a tree, motioning
VERB (PAST TENSE)

for quiet. Then Yasha saw it: a thin _____ stretched tight
NOUN

across the path. Someone had _____ a trap!
VERB (PAST TENSE)

_____ from side to side, Beau and Yasha could
VERB ENDING IN "ING"

make out at least six thieves crouched behind bushes and _____.
PLURAL NOUN

Beau shrugged her _____ at Yasha and whispered,
PART OF THE BODY (PLURAL)

"Hey, wanna get some exercise?" "The quiet walk was nice," Yasha said,

drawing her _____ from its scabbard, "but yes, let's." So
NOUN

Beau grinned and _____ the trap. _____
VERB (PAST TENSE)   NUMBER

minutes later, Beau and Yasha emerged from the woods, sweaty, dusty,

and _____. " _____," said Beau, picking
ADJECTIVE   EXCLAMATION

_____ out of Yasha's hair, "that was a great walk." "It was,"
PLURAL NOUN

Yasha said. "We should _____ that more often."
VERB

From CRITICAL ROLE MAD LIBS® • © 2022 by Gilmore's Glorious Goods LLC. All Rights Reserved.
Published by Mad Libs, an imprint of Penguin Random House LLC, 2022

MAD LIBS® is fun to play with friends, but you can also play it by yourself! To begin with, DO NOT look at the story on the page below. Fill in the blanks on this page with the words called for. Then, using the words you have selected, fill in the blank spaces in the story.

Now you've created your own hilarious MAD LIBS® game!

SPRINKLE'S BIG DAY

NOUN _____

ADJECTIVE _____

ARTICLE OF CLOTHING _____

VERB _____

NOUN _____

ANIMAL (PLURAL) _____

VERB _____

TYPE OF FOOD _____

A PLACE _____

VERB _____

ADJECTIVE _____

NOUN _____

TYPE OF LIQUID _____

VERB (PAST TENSE) _____

NOUN _____

ANIMAL _____

VERB _____

MAD LIBS

SPRINKLE'S BIG DAY

A typical day in the _____ of Sprinkle, Jester's pet, who is,
NOUN

without a doubt, a completely _____ weasel:
ADJECTIVE

Dawn: wake up in Jester's _____, stretch, and
ARTICLE OF CLOTHING

_____ for the day
VERB

Breakfast: eat _____ wrapped in pocket bacon
NOUN

Midmorning: hide during battle with giant _____;
ANIMAL (PLURAL)

try to _____ lollipop and fail (again)
VERB

Lunch: enjoy _____ (not the lollipop)
TYPE OF FOOD

Midafternoon: get dragged into underwater adventure to (the)

_____; _____ breath for as long as possible
A PLACE   *VERB*

Dinner: nibble on _____ crumbs from a/an _____
ADJECTIVE   *NOUN*

in Jester's pocket; drink lots of _____
TYPE OF LIQUID

Sunset: more battle-time hiding; get lightly _____ by a
VERB (PAST TENSE)

fireball

Snack: eat toasted _____ and roasted _____
NOUN   *ANIMAL*

Bedtime: settle down for the night; wonder what could possibly

_____ tomorrow
VERB

From CRITICAL ROLE MAD LIBS® • © 2022 by Gilmore's Glorious Goods LLC. All Rights Reserved.
Published by Mad Libs, an imprint of Penguin Random House LLC, 2022

MAD LIBS® is fun to play with friends, but you can also play it by yourself! To begin with, DO NOT look at the story on the page below. Fill in the blanks on this page with the words called for. Then, using the words you have selected, fill in the blank spaces in the story.

Now you've created your own hilarious MAD LIBS® game!

AND THAT'S WHERE WE'LL LEAVE IT FOR TONIGHT

OCCUPATION _____

SILLY WORD _____

ADVERB _____

VERB _____

EXCLAMATION _____

VERB ENDING IN "ING" _____

NUMBER _____

SAME OCCUPATION _____

VERB _____

PART OF THE BODY (PLURAL) _____

NOUN _____

VERB ENDING IN "ING" _____

VERB _____

NOUN _____

VERB _____

NOUN _____

ADJECTIVE _____

VERB _____

MAD LIBS®
AND THAT'S WHERE WE'LL LEAVE IT FOR TONIGHT

" . . . And the _____ reveals," Matt says, "that her real name is
_____OCCUPATION_____

_____." He pauses _____, then finishes, "And that's
___SILLY WORD___   ___ADVERB___

where we'll _____ it for tonight!" "_____!"
_____VERB_____   ___EXCLAMATION___

yells Travis. "We can't stop _____ *now*," says Ashley. "I
_____VERB ENDING IN "ING"_____

know it's been _____ hours," Liam says, "but what if we went
_____NUMBER_____

just a little longer?" "Wait, guys," Sam puts in, "you know who that

_____ was, right?" The other players _____
___SAME OCCUPATION___   ___VERB___

their heads. Then Marisha's _____ go wide.
_____PART OF THE BODY (PLURAL)_____

"Was that my _____?" she asks. "No *way*," Laura gasps,
_____NOUN_____

_____ up from the table. "But didn't she _____?"
___VERB ENDING IN "ING"___   ___VERB___

asks Taliesin. "Technically," Matt says, grinning, "but they never found

her _____." What a cliffhanger to _____
_____NOUN_____   _____VERB_____

the episode on! No one wants to wait a whole _____ to
_____NOUN_____

play again, but it's time to head home. "Have a/an _____ week,"
_____ADJECTIVE_____

Matt says to the camera. "We _____ you very much, and is it
_____VERB_____

Thursday yet?"

Join the millions of Mad Libs fans
creating wacky and wonderful
stories on our apps!
Download **Mad Libs** today!